THE
UNITED
STATES
PRESIDENTS

BILL CLINTON

BreAnn Rumsch

**Checkerboard
Library**

An Imprint of Abdo Publishing
abdobooks.com

ABDOBOOKS.COM

Published by Abdo Publishing, a division of ABDO, PO Box 398166, Minneapolis, Minnesota 55439.

Printed in the United States of America, North Mankato, Minnesota
052020
092020

 THIS BOOK CONTAINS RECYCLED MATERIALS

Design: Emily O'Malley, Kelly Doudna, Mighty Media, Inc.
Production: Mighty Media, Inc.
Editor: Liz Salzmann

Cover Photograph: Getty Images
Interior Photographs: Albert de Bruijn/iStockphoto, p. 37; AP Images, pp. 6, 7, 15, 17, 18, 20, 21, 22, 26, 27, 28, 30, 31, 36; Arnold Sachs/Getty Images, p. 12; BOB DAEMMRICH/Getty Images, p. 19; Cameron Davidson/Alamy, p. 13; Clinton Presidential Library, pp. 6 (Clinton on pony), 10, 11; DAVID AKE/Getty Images, p. 23; Getty Images, p. 14; Library of Congress, pp. 25, 40; LUKE FRAZZA/Getty Images, p. 29; Pete Souza/Flickr, p. 44; Shutterstock Images, pp. 7 (Hillary campaign), 38, 39; Terry Smith Images' Arkansas Picture Library/Alamy, p. 32; Wikimedia Commons, pp. 5, 40 (George Washington), 42; Win McNamee/Getty Images, p. 33

Library of Congress Control Number: 2019956429

Publisher's Cataloging-in-Publication Data
Names: Rumsch, BreAnn, author.
Title: Bill Clinton / by BreAnn Rumsch
Description: Minneapolis, Minnesota : Abdo Publishing, 2021 | Series: The United States presidents | Includes online resources and index.
Identifiers: ISBN 9781532193453 (lib. bdg.) | ISBN 9781098212094 (ebook)
Subjects: LCSH: Clinton, Bill, 1946---Juvenile literature. | Presidents--Biography--Juvenile literature. | Presidents--United States--History--Juvenile literature. | Legislators--United States--Biography--Juvenile literature. | Politics and government--Biography--Juvenile literature.
Classification: DDC 973.929092--dc23

★ CONTENTS ★

Bill Clinton 4

Timeline 6

Did You Know? 9

Early Years 10

A Future Leader 12

Law and Marriage 14

Governor Clinton 16

Return to Politics 18

President Clinton 20

President Clinton's Cabinet .24

Second Term 26

Impeachment 30

Moving On 32

Office of the President 34

Presidents and Their Terms 40

Glossary 46

Online Resources 47

Index 48

Bill Clinton

Bill Clinton was the forty-second president of the United States. His interest in politics began at a young age. In high school, he participated in government clubs. Then in college, he served as class president.

After college, Clinton taught law school. Then, he was elected **attorney general** of Arkansas. Clinton later served five terms as governor of Arkansas.

In 1993, Clinton became president. As president, he worked hard to improve the **economy**. Clinton also helped make peace in other nations.

President Clinton's popularity won him a second term. Yet, he faced personal **scandals** that led to his **impeachment** in 1998. Still, he continued to work hard for Americans.

After leaving the White House, Clinton remained active in many worthy causes. He started the William J. Clinton Foundation in 2001. Then in 2004, he opened the William J. Clinton Presidential Center.

1963

Clinton became interested in a political career after meeting President John F. Kennedy.

1973

Clinton graduated from Yale Law School in New Haven, Connecticut.

1976

Clinton was elected attorney general of Arkansas.

1980

Clinton's daughter, Chelsea, was born.

1946

On August 19, William Jefferson Clinton was born in Hope, Arkansas.

1975

On October 11, Clinton married Hillary Diane Rodham.

1979

Clinton became governor of Arkansas.

1968

Clinton graduated from Georgetown University in Washington, DC.

1994

On January 1, the North American Free Trade Agreement took effect. Kenneth Starr began investigating the Whitewater affair.

1998

The US House of Representatives impeached Clinton in December.

1996

President Clinton was elected to a second term.

2004

Clinton published his autobiography called *My Life*. In November, the William J. Clinton Presidential Center opened in Little Rock, Arkansas.

★ ★ ★ ★ ★ ★ ★ ★

1993

On January 20, Clinton became the forty-second US president. Congress passed the Brady Handgun Violence Prevention Act and the Family and Medical Leave Act.

2007

Clinton published the book *Giving: How Each of Us Can Change the World*.

1999

On February 12, the US Senate found Clinton not guilty.

2016

Clinton supported Hillary's campaign for US president.

"There is nothing wrong with America that cannot be cured **by what is right with America.**"

BILL CLINTON

DID YOU KNOW?

- ★ Bill Clinton enjoys many hobbies. He stays active by jogging and golfing. He also likes to read, solve crossword puzzles, and play the tenor saxophone.

- ★ Inaugurated at age 46, Clinton became the third-youngest person to serve as US president. John F. Kennedy and Theodore Roosevelt were younger when they were inaugurated. Kennedy was 43 and Roosevelt was just 42.

- ★ In 1996, Clinton became the first Democratic president reelected in 60 years. Back in 1936, Democrat Franklin D. Roosevelt was elected to his second of four terms.

- ★ In 2000, Clinton appointed Norman Mineta secretary of commerce. Mineta was the first Asian American to serve in a US president's cabinet.

Early Years

William Jefferson Clinton was born on August 19, 1946, in Hope, Arkansas. He was called Billy when he was young. Billy's mother, Virginia Dell Blythe, named him William Jefferson Blythe III after his father. His father had died in a car accident three months before Billy was born.

When Billy was two, his mother moved to New Orleans, Louisiana, to attend nursing school. Virginia left Billy in Hope. He stayed with her parents, Eldridge and Edith Cassidy. Billy's grandparents ran a grocery store in Hope. They took good care of Billy. They also taught him to count and read.

★ FAST FACTS

BORN: August 19, 1946

WIFE: Hillary Diane Rodham (1947–)

CHILDREN: 1

POLITICAL PARTY: Democrat

AGE AT INAUGURATION: 46

YEARS SERVED: 1993–2001

VICE PRESIDENT: Al Gore

Billy at age three

Virginia returned to Hope when Billy was four. Shortly after, she married a car dealer named Roger Clinton. In 1953, the family moved to Hot Springs, Arkansas. There, Roger and Virginia had a son named Roger.

Billy's home life was hard. His stepfather drank too much and sometimes hurt Virginia. So in April 1962, Virginia

Billy (*left*), his mother, and his brother, Roger

divorced Roger. But later that summer, they remarried. Billy wanted to share his family's last name. So, he changed his last name from Blythe to Clinton. He also began to go by Bill.

A Future Leader

In Hot Springs, Bill attended Hot Springs High School. He was a busy student and a good musician. Bill played saxophone in the school band. He also competed in band festivals, where he won many medals. Every summer, Bill attended band camp in Fayetteville, Arkansas.

Bill also participated in student government. He belonged to the American Legion Boys Nation. This club is for students interested in government.

Bill visited Washington, DC, with the Boys Nation in 1963. While there, he shook hands with President John F. Kennedy. Bill knew then that he wanted a life in politics.

In 1964, Bill graduated from high school. Then he attended Georgetown University in Washington, DC. There, Bill studied international affairs.

Bill considered President Kennedy his hero.

Georgetown University sits on the
banks of the Potomac River.

At Georgetown, Bill served as class president two years in a row. He also worked as an **intern** for Arkansas senator J. William Fulbright. In 1968, Bill graduated.

That fall, Bill began attending Oxford University in England. As a **Rhodes scholar**, he studied there for two years. Then, Bill traveled around Europe before returning to the United States.

Law and Marriage

In 1970, Clinton went to Yale Law School in New Haven, Connecticut. In addition to studying, he worked as a lawyer's assistant. He also taught a law class at the University of New Haven. Clinton graduated from Yale in 1973.

That spring, Clinton passed his examination to become a lawyer. Then he moved to Fayetteville, Arkansas. He took a job teaching at the University of Arkansas School of Law.

Clinton met Hillary at the
Yale University library.

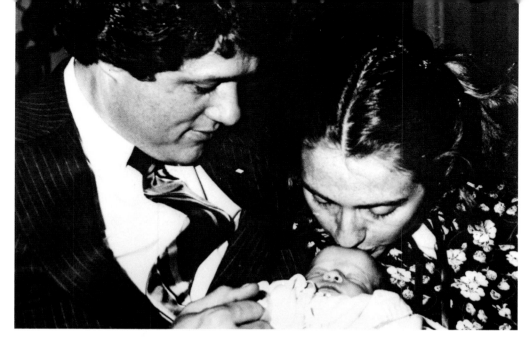

Chelsea is Mr. and Mrs. Clinton's only child.

In 1974, Clinton ran for the US House of Representatives. He lost the race, so he continued to teach law. Clinton also stayed interested in politics.

While at Yale, Clinton had met Hillary Diane Rodham. She had been a law student too. Together, they had worked on **Democratic** senator George McGovern's 1972 presidential campaign. The two had grown close. They married on October 11, 1975. Eventually, the Clintons had a daughter. Chelsea was born in 1980.

Governor Clinton

In 1976, Clinton ran for Arkansas **attorney general** and **won**. He held this position for two years. Then in 1978, Clinton ran for governor of Arkansas. He won! The next year, Clinton became the youngest governor the country had seen in 40 years.

Governor Clinton had many ideas for new programs. One was to repair and improve the roads in the state. To pay for this, Clinton raised taxes and fees. This upset voters.

Clinton had other problems too. He upset logging companies by saying they harvested too many Arkansas forests. Voters were also angry because of the thousands of Cuban **refugees** Clinton allowed to come to Arkansas. Some of the refugees started **riots**. The riots caused injuries and property damage.

In 1980, Governor Clinton ran for reelection. Voters were still upset with him, so he did not win. After the election, Clinton returned to practicing law. He joined the firm of Wright, Lindsey, and Jennings in Little Rock, Arkansas.

As attorney general, Clinton supported the interests of consumers.

Return to Politics

Clinton still wanted to work in politics. So, he ran for governor again in 1982. This time, he said he had learned from his mistakes. The voters believed him and voted him into office. Clinton went on to be reelected three more times.

Clinton announced his candidacy for president on October 3, 1991. He and Gore (*left*) were elected on November 3, 1992.

Governor Clinton supported laws to improve education. Soon, teachers were tested to be sure they knew their subjects well. Parents received fines if they did not attend parent-teacher conferences. And, any student who quit school lost his or her driver's license.

Governor Clinton improved the **economy** too. He worked on laws that drew businesses to Arkansas. Soon, there were many well-paying jobs. Clinton also developed a new plan for welfare. It provided job training for those receiving welfare benefits.

President George H.W. Bush

Clinton was now known nationwide. So in 1992, the **Democratic** Party nominated him for president. Clinton chose Tennessee senator Al Gore as his **running mate**. **Republicans** renominated President George H.W. Bush and Vice President Dan Quayle.

Voters were upset with Bush because of the poor national economy. So, Clinton won the election! He earned 370 electoral votes, while Bush received only 168.

President Clinton

Clinton took office on January 20, 1993. Congress soon passed many laws Clinton supported. The Brady Handgun Violence Prevention Act passed in 1993. This bill tightened gun control laws.

Another important law was the Family and Medical Leave Act. This allowed employees time off to care for a new baby or a sick family member.

At Clinton's inauguration, he emphasized the importance of individuals taking responsibility to make the country a better place.

President Clinton signed the Family and Medical Leave Act on February 5, 1993.

Then in September, Clinton suggested ways to improve America's health care system. His plan would allow all Americans to get health **insurance**. However, Congress voted against Clinton's plan.

Clinton also worked on the North American Free Trade Agreement (NAFTA). It took effect on January 1, 1994. NAFTA slowly ended **tariffs** on goods exchanged between the United States, Mexico, and Canada. This greatly improved trade.

Clinton encouraged peace talks between Israeli prime minister Yitzhak Rabin (*left*) and Palestine Liberation Organization chairman Yasir Arafat (*right*).

President Clinton worked with other countries too. In 1993, he had invited leaders from Israel and Palestine to sign a peace agreement. Then in 1994, Clinton sent US troops to Haiti. They returned Haiti's president to power after he had been overthrown. In 1995, Clinton sent US troops to Bosnia to help maintain peace.

Meanwhile, the Clintons faced personal problems. They had invested in some Arkansas property

SUPREME COURT APPOINTMENTS

RUTH BADER GINSBURG: 1993
STEPHEN G. BREYER: 1994

with the Whitewater Development Corporation. But some people believed the land deals were illegal.

In 1994, the US government hired lawyer Kenneth Starr to investigate the case. Clinton **testified** on videotape, which was shown to Congress. His business partners were found guilty in May 1996. But the charges against the Clintons were dropped. This **scandal** became known as the Whitewater affair.

Dole received just 159 electoral votes to Clinton's 379.

That same year, President Clinton and Vice President Gore ran for reelection. The **Republican** Party nominated Senator Bob Dole of Kansas for president. Former congressman Jack Kemp became his **running mate**. Times were good, so voters did not want a change. Clinton easily won the election.

PRESIDENT CLINTON'S CABINET

FIRST TERM
January 20, 1993–January 20, 1997

- ★ **STATE:** Warren M. Christopher
- ★ **TREASURY:** Lloyd Bentsen Jr.
Robert E. Rubin (from January 10, 1995)
- ★ **ATTORNEY GENERAL:** Janet Reno
- ★ **INTERIOR:** Bruce Babbitt
- ★ **AGRICULTURE:** Mike Espy
Dan Glickman (from March 30, 1995)
- ★ **COMMERCE:** Ronald H. Brown
Mickey Kantor (from April 12, 1996)
- ★ **LABOR:** Robert B. Reich
- ★ **DEFENSE:** Les Aspin
William J. Perry (from February 3, 1994)
- ★ **HEALTH AND HUMAN SERVICES:**
Donna E. Shalala
- ★ **HOUSING AND URBAN DEVELOPMENT:**
Henry G. Cisneros
- ★ **TRANSPORTATION:** Federico Peña
- ★ **ENERGY:** Hazel R. O'Leary
- ★ **EDUCATION:** Richard W. Riley
- ★ **VETERANS AFFAIRS:** Jesse Brown

SECOND TERM
January 20, 1997–January 20, 2001

- ★ **STATE:** Madeleine Albright
- ★ **TREASURY:** Robert E. Rubin
Lawrence H. Summers (from July 2, 1999)
- ★ **ATTORNEY GENERAL:** Janet Reno
- ★ **INTERIOR:** Bruce Babbitt
- ★ **AGRICULTURE:** Dan Glickman
- ★ **COMMERCE:** William M. Daley
Norman Mineta (from July 21, 2000)
- ★ **LABOR:** Alexis M. Herman
- ★ **DEFENSE:** William Cohen
- ★ **HEALTH AND HUMAN SERVICES:**
Donna E. Shalala
- ★ **HOUSING AND URBAN DEVELOPMENT:**
Andrew M. Cuomo
- ★ **TRANSPORTATION:** Rodney Slater
- ★ **ENERGY:** Federico Peña
Bill Richardson (from August 18, 1998)
- ★ **EDUCATION:** Richard W. Riley
- ★ **VETERANS AFFAIRS:** Togo D. West Jr.
Hershel W. Gober (from July 25, 2000)

Clinton (*left*) looks on while the members
of his cabinet are sworn in.

Second Term

During Clinton's second term, America faced conflicts in other countries. In 1998, **terrorists** based in Afghanistan bombed US **embassies** in Africa. Clinton ordered military attacks against the terrorists.

In 1999, the Clintons traveled to Europe. Clinton spoke to NATO troops helping with the conflict in Kosovo.

At the same time, Iraq would not let the **United Nations (UN)** inspect its weapons factories. The UN feared Iraq was making dangerous weapons. So, President Clinton ordered military attacks against Iraq.

Meanwhile, Yugoslavia had been attacking people in Kosovo. In March 1999, Clinton supported attacks on Yugoslavia by **NATO**. By June, Yugoslavia agreed to stop the fighting. So, NATO stopped its attacks. It also sent troops to Kosovo to keep the peace. About 7,000 American soldiers joined the effort.

Madeleine Albright

Back home, Clinton had named Madeleine Albright **secretary of state** in 1996. The next year, she became the first woman to head the Department of State. Clinton also named Bill Richardson as America's head delegate to the UN. Richardson was the first Hispanic to hold this job.

President Clinton also worked to decrease government spending. During this time, the **economy** continued to grow. For the first time since 1969, the government had a budget **surplus**. And by 1998, many more people had jobs and owned their own homes.

Meanwhile, Clinton had additional personal problems.

Bill Richardson

Back in 1994, a woman named Paula Jones had filed a **lawsuit** against him. A judge dismissed the case in April 1998. However, Jones appealed the case. And, Kenneth Starr wanted to investigate Clinton further.

On August 17, 1998, Clinton appeared before a **grand jury**. He swore to tell the truth. Clinton then settled the Jones lawsuit in November. But his problems were not over.

Starr served as independent counsel while investigating Clinton. This type of lawyer helps trials that involve political parties remain fair.

Impeachment

Starr had sent a report to the US House of Representatives in September. It said Clinton may have lied to the **grand jury**. Lying in court is a crime called perjury.

So in December 1998, the House of Representatives **impeached** Clinton. The House passed two articles of impeachment. One said Clinton may have committed perjury. The other said Clinton may have asked others to lie too. This is called obstruction of justice.

The House delivered this binder to the Senate. It contained the articles of impeachment.

Next, the US Senate held a trial. They tried to figure out if Clinton was guilty of the two articles. They also tried to decide if Clinton should lose his job as president. On February 12, 1999, the Senate found Clinton not guilty. So, he was allowed to remain president.

In 2000, Hillary Clinton was elected to the US Senate by the people of New York.

Moving On

In January 2001, the Clintons left the White House and moved to New York. That year, Clinton started the William J. Clinton Foundation. It addresses problems such as **AIDS**, poverty, and **climate change**. The organization was later renamed the Clinton Foundation.

In 2004, Clinton published his **autobiography**. It was called *My Life*. That November, the William J. Clinton Presidential Center opened in Little Rock. It includes a library and a museum.

Clinton and former president George H.W. Bush joined efforts in 2005. Together, they worked to raise money for victims of natural **disasters**. Then in 2007, Clinton published the book *Giving: How Each of Us Can Change the World*.

In 2008 and 2016, Clinton had a new role in politics. Both years, Hillary Clinton

The William J. Clinton
Presidential Center

Clinton often travels to parts of the world where
the Clinton Foundation offers support.

ran for US president. Clinton gave many speeches on
his wife's behalf. In 2008, Hillary withdrew from the
race to support Barack Obama. In 2016, Hillary won the
Democratic nomination. However, she lost the election to
Donald Trump.

During his presidency, Clinton worked hard to improve
social problems and the **economy**. Today, Bill Clinton
remains devoted to making the world a better place.

BRANCHES OF GOVERNMENT

The US government is divided into three branches. They are the executive, legislative, and judicial branches. This division is called a separation of powers. Each branch has some power over the others. This is called a system of checks and balances.

★ EXECUTIVE BRANCH

The executive branch enforces laws. It is made up of the president, the vice president, and the president's cabinet. The president represents the United States around the world. He or she oversees relations with other countries and signs treaties. The president signs bills into law and appoints officials and federal judges. He or she also leads the military and manages government workers.

★ LEGISLATIVE BRANCH

The legislative branch makes laws, maintains the military, and regulates trade. It also has the power to declare war. This branch consists of the Senate and the House of Representatives. Together, these two houses make up Congress. Each state has two senators. A state's population determines the number of representatives it has.

★ JUDICIAL BRANCH

The judicial branch interprets laws. It consists of district courts, courts of appeals, and the Supreme Court. District courts try cases. If a person disagrees with a trial's outcome, he or she may appeal. If a court of appeals supports the ruling, a person may appeal to the Supreme Court. The Supreme Court also makes sure that laws follow the US Constitution.

THE PRESIDENT ★

★ QUALIFICATIONS FOR OFFICE

To be president, a person must meet three requirements. A candidate must be at least 35 years old and a natural-born US citizen. He or she must also have lived in the United States for at least 14 years.

★ ELECTORAL COLLEGE

The US presidential election is an indirect election. Voters from each state choose electors to represent them in the Electoral College. The number of electors from each state is based on the state's population. Each elector has one electoral vote. Electors are pledged to cast their vote for the candidate who receives the highest number of popular votes in their state. A candidate must receive the majority of Electoral College votes to win.

★ TERM OF OFFICE

Each president may be elected to two four-year terms. Sometimes, a president may only be elected once. This happens if he or she served more than two years of the previous president's term.

The presidential election is held on the Tuesday after the first Monday in November. The president is sworn in on January 20 of the following year. At that time, he or she takes the oath of office:

> *I do solemnly swear (or affirm) that I will faithfully execute the office of President of the United States, and will to the best of my ability, preserve, protect and defend the Constitution of the United States.*

LINE OF SUCCESSION

The Presidential Succession Act of 1947 defines who becomes president if the president cannot serve. The vice president is first in the line of succession. Next are the Speaker of the House and the President Pro Tempore of the Senate. If none of these individuals is able to serve, the office falls to the president's cabinet members. They would take office in the order in which each department was created:

Secretary of State

Secretary of the Treasury

Secretary of Defense

Attorney General

Secretary of the Interior

Secretary of Agriculture

Secretary of Commerce

Secretary of Labor

Secretary of Health and Human Services

Secretary of Housing and Urban Development

Secretary of Transportation

Secretary of Energy

Secretary of Education

Secretary of Veterans Affairs

Secretary of Homeland Security

While in office, the president receives a salary of $400,000 each year. He or she lives in the White House and has 24-hour Secret Service protection.

The president may travel on a Boeing 747 jet called Air Force One. The airplane can accommodate 76 passengers. It has kitchens, a dining room, sleeping areas, and a conference room. It also has fully equipped offices with the latest communications systems. Air Force One can fly halfway around the world before needing to refuel. It can even refuel in flight!

Air Force One

If the president wishes to travel by car, he or she uses Cadillac One. It has been modified with heavy armor and communications systems. The president takes

Cadillac One

Cadillac One along when visiting other countries if secure transportation will be needed.

The president also travels on a helicopter called Marine One. Like the presidential car, Marine One accompanies the president when traveling abroad if necessary.

Sometimes, the president needs to get away and relax with family and friends. Camp David is the official presidential retreat. It is located in the cool, wooded mountains of Maryland. The US Navy maintains the retreat, and the US Marine Corps keeps it secure. The camp offers swimming, tennis, golf, and hiking.

When the president leaves office, he or she receives lifetime Secret Service protection. He or she also receives a yearly pension of $207,800 and funding for office space, supplies, and staff.

Marine One

George Washington

Abraham Lincoln

Theodore Roosevelt

	PRESIDENT	PARTY	TOOK OFFICE
1	George Washington	None	April 30, 1789
2	John Adams	Federalist	March 4, 1797
3	Thomas Jefferson	Democratic-Republican	March 4, 1801
4	James Madison	Democratic-Republican	March 4, 1809
5	James Monroe	Democratic-Republican	March 4, 1817
6	John Quincy Adams	Democratic-Republican	March 4, 1825
7	Andrew Jackson	Democrat	March 4, 1829
8	Martin Van Buren	Democrat	March 4, 1837
9	William H. Harrison	Whig	March 4, 1841
10	John Tyler	Whig	April 6, 1841
11	James K. Polk	Democrat	March 4, 1845
12	Zachary Taylor	Whig	March 5, 1849
13	Millard Fillmore	Whig	July 10, 1850
14	Franklin Pierce	Democrat	March 4, 1853
15	James Buchanan	Democrat	March 4, 1857
16	Abraham Lincoln	Republican	March 4, 1861
17	Andrew Johnson	Democrat	April 15, 1865
18	Ulysses S. Grant	Republican	March 4, 1869
19	Rutherford B. Hayes	Republican	March 3, 1877

THEIR TERMS ★

LEFT OFFICE	TERMS SERVED	VICE PRESIDENT
March 4, 1797	Two	John Adams
March 4, 1801	One	Thomas Jefferson
March 4, 1809	Two	Aaron Burr, George Clinton
March 4, 1817	Two	George Clinton, Elbridge Gerry
March 4, 1825	Two	Daniel D. Tompkins
March 4, 1829	One	John C. Calhoun
March 4, 1837	Two	John C. Calhoun, Martin Van Buren
March 4, 1841	One	Richard M. Johnson
April 4, 1841	Died During First Term	John Tyler
March 4, 1845	Completed Harrison's Term	Office Vacant
March 4, 1849	One	George M. Dallas
July 9, 1850	Died During First Term	Millard Fillmore
March 4, 1853	Completed Taylor's Term	Office Vacant
March 4, 1857	One	William R.D. King
March 4, 1861	One	John C. Breckinridge
April 15, 1865	Served One Term, Died During Second Term	Hannibal Hamlin, Andrew Johnson
March 4, 1869	Completed Lincoln's Second Term	Office Vacant
March 4, 1877	Two	Schuyler Colfax, Henry Wilson
March 4, 1881	One	William A. Wheeler

Franklin D. Roosevelt

John F. Kennedy

Ronald Reagan

	PRESIDENT	PARTY	TOOK OFFICE
20	James A. Garfield	Republican	March 4, 1881
21	Chester Arthur	Republican	September 20, 1881
22	Grover Cleveland	Democrat	March 4, 1885
23	Benjamin Harrison	Republican	March 4, 1889
24	Grover Cleveland	Democrat	March 4, 1893
25	William McKinley	Republican	March 4, 1897
26	Theodore Roosevelt	Republican	September 14, 1901
27	William Taft	Republican	March 4, 1909
28	Woodrow Wilson	Democrat	March 4, 1913
29	Warren G. Harding	Republican	March 4, 1921
30	Calvin Coolidge	Republican	August 3, 1923
31	Herbert Hoover	Republican	March 4, 1929
32	Franklin D. Roosevelt	Democrat	March 4, 1933
33	Harry S. Truman	Democrat	April 12, 1945
34	Dwight D. Eisenhower	Republican	January 20, 1953
35	John F. Kennedy	Democrat	January 20, 1961

★ ★ ★

LEFT OFFICE	TERMS SERVED	VICE PRESIDENT
September 19, 1881	Died During First Term	Chester Arthur
March 4, 1885	Completed Garfield's Term	Office Vacant
March 4, 1889	One	Thomas A. Hendricks
March 4, 1893	One	Levi P. Morton
March 4, 1897	One	Adlai E. Stevenson
September 14, 1901	Served One Term, Died During Second Term	Garret A. Hobart, Theodore Roosevelt
March 4, 1909	Completed McKinley's Second Term, Served One Term	Office Vacant, Charles Fairbanks
March 4, 1913	One	James S. Sherman
March 4, 1921	Two	Thomas R. Marshall
August 2, 1923	Died During First Term	Calvin Coolidge
March 4, 1929	Completed Harding's Term, Served One Term	Office Vacant, Charles Dawes
March 4, 1933	One	Charles Curtis
April 12, 1945	Served Three Terms, Died During Fourth Term	John Nance Garner, Henry A. Wallace, Harry S. Truman
January 20, 1953	Completed Roosevelt's Fourth Term, Served One Term	Office Vacant, Alben Barkley
January 20, 1961	Two	Richard Nixon
November 22, 1963	Died During First Term	Lyndon B. Johnson

	PRESIDENT	PARTY	TOOK OFFICE
36	Lyndon B. Johnson	Democrat	November 22, 1963
37	Richard Nixon	Republican	January 20, 1969
38	Gerald Ford	Republican	August 9, 1974
39	Jimmy Carter	Democrat	January 20, 1977
40	Ronald Reagan	Republican	January 20, 1981
41	George H.W. Bush	Republican	January 20, 1989
42	Bill Clinton	Democrat	January 20, 1993
43	George W. Bush	Republican	January 20, 2001
44	Barack Obama	Democrat	January 20, 2009
45	Donald Trump	Republican	January 20, 2017

Barack Obama

★ PRESIDENTS MATH GAME ★

Have fun with this presidents math game! First, study the list above and memorize each president's name and number. Then, use math to figure out which president completes each equation below.

1. Bill Clinton − Warren G. Harding = ?

2. George Washington + Bill Clinton = ?

3. Bill Clinton − William H. Harrison = ?

Answers: 1. Millard Fillmore (42 − 29 = 13)
2. George W. Bush (1 + 42 = 43)
3. Harry S. Truman (42 − 9 = 33)

LEFT OFFICE	TERMS SERVED	VICE PRESIDENT
January 20, 1969	Completed Kennedy's Term, Served One Term	Office Vacant, Hubert H. Humphrey
August 9, 1974	Completed First Term, Resigned During Second Term	Spiro T. Agnew, Gerald Ford
January 20, 1977	Completed Nixon's Second Term	Nelson A. Rockefeller
January 20, 1981	One	Walter Mondale
January 20, 1989	Two	George H.W. Bush
January 20, 1993	One	Dan Quayle
January 20, 2001	Two	Al Gore
January 20, 2009	Two	Dick Cheney
January 20, 2017	Two	Joe Biden
		Mike Pence

★ WRITE TO THE PRESIDENT ★

You may write to the president at:

The White House
1600 Pennsylvania Avenue NW
Washington, DC 20500

You may email the president at:

www.whitehouse.gov/contact

★ GLOSSARY ★

AIDS—Acquired Immune Deficiency Syndrome. A disease that weakens the immune system. It is caused by the Human Immunodeficiency Virus (HIV).

attorney general—the chief law officer of a national or state government.

autobiography—a story of a person's life that is written by himself or herself.

climate change—a long-term change in Earth's climate, or in that of a region of Earth. It includes changing temperatures, weather patterns, and more. It can result from natural processes or human activities.

Democrat—a member of the Democratic political party. Democrats believe in social change and strong government.

disaster—a sudden event that causes destruction and suffering or loss of life. Natural disasters include events such as hurricanes, tornadoes, and earthquakes.

economy—the way a nation uses its money, goods, and natural resources.

embassy—the home and office of a diplomat who lives in a foreign country.

grand jury—a group of people who investigate a crime. The group decides if there is enough evidence for a trial.

impeach—to charge a public official with misconduct in office.

insurance—a contract that helps people pay their bills if they are sick or hurt. People with insurance pay money each month to keep the contract.

intern—an advanced student or graduate gaining supervised practical experience in his or her field.

lawsuit—a case held before a court.

NATO—North Atlantic Treaty Organization. A group formed by the United States, Canada, and some European countries in 1949. It tries to create peace among its nations and protect them from common enemies.

refugee—a person who flees to another country for safety and protection.

Republican—a member of the Republican political party. Republicans are conservative and believe in small government.

Rhodes scholar—a student who has a scholarship to Oxford University. It is given to students with good grades who have shown leadership.

riot—a sometimes violent disturbance caused by a large group of people.

running mate—a candidate running for a lower-rank position on an election ticket, especially the candidate for vice president.

scandal—an action that shocks people and disgraces those connected with it.

secretary of state—a member of the president's cabinet who handles relations with other countries.

surplus—an amount above what is needed.

tariff—the taxes a government puts on imported or exported goods.

terrorist—a person who uses violence to threaten people or governments.

testify—to speak under oath in a court of law.

United Nations (UN)—a group of nations formed in 1945. Its goals are peace, human rights, security, and social and economic development.

ONLINE RESOURCES

Booklinks
NONFICTION NETWORK
FREE! ONLINE NONFICTION RESOURCES

To learn more about Bill Clinton, please visit **abdobooklinks.com** or scan this QR code. These links are routinely monitored and updated to provide the most current information available.

★ INDEX ★

A

Albright, Madeleine, 27

American Legion Boys Nation, 12

Arkansas attorney general, 4, 16

B

birth, 10

Brady Handgun Violence Prevention Act, 20

Bush, George H.W., 19, 32

C

childhood, 4, 10, 11, 12

Clinton Foundation, 4, 32

Congress, US, 20, 21, 23

D

Democratic Party, 15, 19, 33

Dole, Bob, 23

E

education, 4, 10, 12, 13, 14

F

family, 10, 11, 15, 22, 23, 32, 33

Family and Medical Leave Act, 20

Fulbright, J. William, 13

G

Giving: How Each of Us Can Change the World, 32

Gore, Al, 19, 23

governor, 4, 16, 18, 19

H

House of Representatives, US, 15, 30

I

impeachment, 4, 30

inauguration, 20

J

Jones, Paula, 28

K

Kemp, Jack, 23

Kennedy, John F., 12

M

McGovern, George, 15

My Life, 32

N

NATO, 27

North American Free Trade Agreement, 21

O

Obama, Barack, 33

Q

Quayle, Dan, 19

R

Republican Party, 19, 23

retirement, 32

Richardson, Bill, 27

S

Senate, US, 30

Starr, Kenneth, 23, 28, 30

T

terrorism, 26

Trump, Donald, 33

U

United Nations (UN), 27

W

Washington, DC, 12

Whitewater affair, 22, 23

William J. Clinton Foundation. *See* Clinton Foundation

William J. Clinton Presidential Center, 4, 32